Bennett, Evelyn,
1950-

Frederick Douglass
and the war against
slavery.

| DATE | | |
|---|---|---|
| | | |
| | | |
| | | |
| | | |
| | | |
| | | |
| | | |
| | | |
| | | |
| | | |
| | | |
| | | |
| | | |
| | | |

# FREDERICK
# DOUGLASS

## and the War Against Slavery

### by Evelyn Bennett

GATEWAY CIVIL RIGHTS
THE MILLBROOK PRESS
BROOKFIELD, CONNECTICUT

*An anti-slavery meeting at Exeter Hall in 1841.*

Photographs courtesy of The Philbrook Museum of Art, Tulsa, Oklahoma: cover; Library of Congress: cover inset, pp. 7, 8, 12–13, 15, 17 (bottom), 24, 26; Bettmann Archive: pp. 1, 2–3, 17 (top), 18, 29; National Portrait Gallery, Smithsonian Institution: p. 4 (NPB.74.74); Museum of the City of New York: p. 10; Moorland-Spingarn Research Center, Howard University: p. 16; American Antiquarian Society: p. 20; The Granger Collection: p. 22; Frederick Douglass Historic Site, National Park Service: p. 30.

Library of Congress Cataloging-in-Publication Data
Bennett, Evelyn, 1950–
Frederick Douglass and the war against slavery
by Evelyn Bennett
p.   cm.—(Gateway civil rights)
Includes bibliographical references (p.    ) and index.
Summary: A biography of the escaped slave who became an orator, writer, and leader in the abolitionist movement in the nineteenth century.
ISBN 1-56294-341-3 (lib. bdg.)
1. Douglass, Frederick, 1817?–1895—Juvenile literature.   2. Abolitionists—United States—Biography—Juvenile literature.   3. Afro-Americans—Biography—Juvenile literature.   4. Slavery—United States—Anti-slavery movements—Juvenile literature.   [1. Douglass, Frederick, 1817?–1895. 2. Abolitionists. 3. Afro-Americans—Biography.] I. Title.   II. Series.
E449.D75B45   1993
973.8′092—dc20      [B]      92-36930   CIP   AC

Published by The Millbrook Press
2 Old New Milford Road, Brookfield, Connecticut 06804

*Frederick Douglass moved many people through his
speeches and writing about the evils of slavery.*

**I**n *the summer of 1841,* a group of people opposed to slavery gathered in a meeting hall on Nantucket, an island off the coast of Massachusetts. After several white speakers finished, a tall young black man was asked to tell the audience about his life as a slave down South. At first he was shy and could barely speak, but the audience cheered him on until his voice gained strength and feeling.

In powerful words, he told how he had been taken away from his mother when he was born, and how he had been nearly starved and often beaten. Then he described how he had taught himself to read and write, and how he had longed for freedom with all his heart and soul. Finally he could stand it no longer and escaped to the North.

When he finished, many people were in tears. Although they were against slavery for religious reasons, most of them had never seen a slave before or heard a firsthand account of a slave's suffering. Listening to the moving story the handsome black man told made them more determined than ever to end slavery. They all vowed that from then on they would help slaves escape, even if it meant breaking the law.

When the meeting was over, a man who was a leader of the anti-slavery movement asked the ex-slave to travel around the country and tell Americans everywhere about the evils of slavery. He agreed.

His name was Frederick Douglass. Just by speaking that day, he was risking his freedom, since as an escaped slave he could be returned to his master if he was caught. Even though slavery was against the law in Massachusetts, it was still legal for Southern slave owners to recapture their "property."

But although he was married and had two young children to support, Frederick Douglass was willing to take that risk in order to speak out against the terrible things he had seen and experienced. He traveled not only around America, but to Britain, too, to rally people to the cause. He also wrote a book about his experiences in the South that opened people's eyes.

All his life, he would fight for the freedom of his race and the rights of people everywhere. He became a newspaper editor, a consultant of President Lincoln's, a United States marshal, a minister to Haiti, and one of the most famous black writers and speakers of his day. He is one of the great figures in the struggle for civil rights.

## The Early Years

The man known as Frederick Douglass was born Frederick Augustus Washington Bailey some time in February 1817. It was a grand-sounding name for a slave. Sadly, his name was the only thing his mother could give him. She worked in the cornfields of Captain Aaron Anthony, plantation manager for one

*A slave is sold away from her baby. Frederick, too,
was separated from his mother at a young age.*

of the richest men in Maryland. Like most slaves, Harriet Bailey was not allowed to look after her son, even though many people said Frederick was Captain Anthony's own child. He would never find out for sure. All he knew was that his father was a white man.

Frederick was sent to live with his grandmother, Betsey Bailey. Too old to be a field hand, she had been given the job of looking after slaves' children in her cabin. Frederick hardly ever saw his mother. She had to walk 12 miles (19 kilometers) to spend a few hours with him after working in the fields all day, and then walk back to start work again at sunrise.

But his years with his loving grandmother were happy ones.

# THE AFRICAN SLAVE TRADE

The African slave trade was already over a hundred years old when a Dutch ship brought twenty Africans to Jamestown, Virginia, in 1619. These were the first Africans sold as slaves in America.

Africans were captured by Arab and European slave traders in three ways. Some traders lay in wait for people and took them prisoner. Others promised African chiefs things like tobacco and liquor if they would make war on another tribe and hand over their prisoners. The third way was for an African chief to offer his own people to the trader in exchange for goods.

These Africans were then forced to walk for days to reach the slave ships, where they were loaded on like animals. Many died on their way to the ships. Many more died of hunger and disease on the ocean voyage. But millions arrived in Europe, the Caribbean, and North and South America, to be sold into slavery.

*Jamestown, Virginia, 1619*

Sometimes she told him about the Old Master, and how he owned Frederick and his mother and grandmother, but the words meant little to the young child. Only when he was about seven, and his grandmother had to deliver him to the Old Master's house, did he begin to understand the terrible meaning of what she had told him.

Frederick's life in Captain Anthony's house was a misery. He and the other slave children were always hungry. They wore rags and did not even have blankets to keep them warm. One night Frederick was awakened by a woman's screams. Peering through a crack in the kitchen wall, he saw Captain Anthony beating his aunt with a whip. It was the first beating he would see, but not the last. Sometimes he himself was whipped. There were some decent slave holders who did not believe in beating slaves, but many were as harsh as Aaron Anthony.

Some members of Anthony's family took a liking to Frederick because he was lively and smart and handsome. Unfortunately, the woman in charge of the slave children hated him for always rebelling against her. One night, his mother showed up at the big house and found this woman about to whip Frederick. She defended him, and then she comforted him and gave him food. It was the last time he would ever see his mother. Shortly afterward, she died.

Frederick's luck improved when he was sent to work for

*Frederick was sent to work for the Auld family here in Baltimore.*

Hugh Auld, a relative of Captain Anthony's who lived in Baltimore. Anthony's daughter gave Frederick his first pair of trousers for the trip, and he was glad to escape from field work. Auld was much nicer, and his wife treated Frederick almost like one of the family. She even began to teach him to read, until her husband stopped her. People felt it was dangerous to teach slaves to read and write, because then they could get ideas about freedom or even forge papers and escape. But Frederick managed to learn by giving poor white children bits of bread to teach him. He began reading anti-slavery works and longing for freedom. Many slaves in Baltimore had been set free by their owners or bought their freedom through their own labor. Why could he not be free, too?

## Escape from Slavery

Before Frederick's dream of freedom could come true, he was sent to other relatives of Captain Anthony's to work as a field hand. Because he would not obey, he was often beaten. He saw how slavery made beasts not only of slaves but of the people who owned them. He also learned that once he fought back, he was less likely to be beaten: "Men are whipped oftenest," he wrote, "who are whipped easiest."

Frederick's first attempt to escape failed when another slave told the authorities, and Frederick was thrown in jail. Shortly afterward, he was sent back to Hugh Auld in Baltimore, who put him to work in a shipyard and gave him only a few dollars out of his pay. But at least Frederick could go to meetings with educated free blacks to prepare for freedom.

During these meetings, Frederick got to know Anna Murray, a free black. She was hardworking, kind, and religious, but not educated. Her peaceful face and long hair made Frederick think of an Indian princess. Soon they were engaged to be married.

Now Frederick wanted his freedom more than ever. So he got his master to let him "hire out" his time after regular working hours and keep some of his pay. With the money he saved and money Anna gave him, he was ready.

# THE FUGITIVE SLAVE LAW

It is estimated that, between 1810 and 1850, as many as 100,000 slaves ran away from their owners and were never recaptured. Many of them used the stations of the Underground Railroad to make their way to the Northern states or Canada; it is said that 40,000 of them passed through Ohio alone. Some of them remained in the South, but managed to get papers that let them pass as free blacks.

It was always risky for anyone to help slaves escape, but the Fugitive Slave Law of 1850 made it much riskier. Anyone who was caught helping a runaway slave could be put in jail or fined one thousand dollars. But many Northerners disobeyed the law anyway. Even Northern policemen often refused to arrest blacks and return them to the South.

The Fugitive Slave Law also meant that a slave catcher could say someone was a runaway slave without having any proof. Captured blacks were not allowed a trial by jury and could not speak out for themselves.

Yet more blacks than ever escaped after the law was passed. The longing for freedom was too strong to be crushed by an act of Congress.

A free black man who also worked at the shipyard lent Frederick his own identification papers. This friend did not look at all like Frederick, so Frederick was scared that when someone read the description on the papers he would be arrested. He boarded the train to Wilmington, Delaware, just as it was leaving. The conductor on the train was too busy to look closely at his papers. Then Frederick saw a white man he knew, but fortunately the man did not say anything.

Finally, after many frightening moments, he arrived in New York City. He had to sleep in the streets that night, behind some barrels, but he did not mind. "A new world had opened upon me," he wrote many years later. Frederick Augustus Washington Bailey would never again be a slave!

## Speaking Out

A friendly sailor Frederick met in New York took him to the home of David Ruggles, a free black. Ruggles was part of the Underground Railroad—a secret network of people who risked their lives and freedom to help runaway slaves escape. The homes where the slaves were hidden on their way to Northern cities or Canada were known as "stations," and the people who helped them were called "conductors." Some of these conductors were black and others were white.

This songbook, published in 1845, shows Frederick Douglass
on his route to freedom, trailed by slave catchers.

*Anna Douglass*

Ruggles hid Frederick from the many slave catchers in New York until he could get a message to Anna. Anna arrived in New York, full of joy, and she and Frederick were married. Soon afterward, Ruggles sent them to stay with another free black in New Bedford, Massachusetts, which had many shipyards like the one where Frederick had worked in Baltimore. In New Bedford, at the suggestion of his new conductor, Frederick Bailey changed his name to Frederick Douglass, so it would be harder for his former master to find him.

As it turned out, he could not get work in the shipyard. The white workers would not let the owner hire skilled blacks. Instead he worked as a ship's loader, as a chimney sweep, and in a factory. He and Anna had two children, a girl named Rosetta and a boy named Lewis Henry. Life was busy, but Douglass went on attending anti-slavery meetings and became involved in the black community.

It was in New Bedford that Douglass first read the *Liberator*, a famous anti-slavery newspaper. Its motto was "Our country is the world—our countrymen are mankind." The *Liberator*'s editor, William Lloyd Garrison, was a white man who had made ending slavery his life's work. He became Douglass's hero. Garrison was one of the leaders of the meeting in Nantucket where Douglass first stood up and spoke.

*William Lloyd Garrison, editor of the* Liberator.

He spoke so well and with such passion that the abolition-ists, as fighters against slavery were called, set up a lecture tour for Douglass throughout New England and in New York and Indiana. Although abolitionists were sometimes beaten and one had even been killed, Douglass knew he had to speak out. He read books and practiced public speaking.

And it worked! Those who heard him were drawn to the handsome black man with his beautiful voice and flashing eyes. In fact, Frederick Douglass was such a fine speaker that some people said he couldn't really be an ex-slave who had never gone to school. It was to stop this rumor that Douglass wrote the story of his life.

*Narrative of the Life of Frederick Douglass* was so powerful that it was read and praised everywhere. Unfortunately, it was also read by Hugh Auld, Doug-lass's former master in Baltimore. He demanded that his slave be recaptured.

Douglass's friends urged him to leave the country. By then he and Anna had four beloved children, whom he hated to leave. Finally, he went to England and Ireland, where his book had sold thousands of copies, and spoke to large crowds.

*This portrait is from* Narrative of the Life of Frederick Douglass, *published in 1845.*

Many English people were so moved by his speeches that they begged him to stay there. But Douglass felt his real place was in America, where there were still slaves who needed help.

When he explained this to his English friends, they raised the money to buy his freedom. They also gave him money to continue his anti-slavery work. After twenty-one months in Europe, Frederick Douglass returned to America in 1847, a free man at last. Nobody could claim to own him but himself.

## The Cause of Freedom

Back in America, Douglass used the money from his English supporters to start publishing an anti-slavery newspaper. He moved his family to Rochester, New York, and his older children all helped him get the paper out. Named for the star that guided blacks to freedom, the *North Star* printed stories and poems by blacks and reported on the fight against slavery. Douglass also used his paper to speak out for women's rights. He believed that "slavery for women is as bad as slavery for Negroes."

At first, hardly anyone bought the *North Star,* but later it attracted many readers. More famous than ever, Douglass continued to travel around the country, delivering lectures. Once he spoke in front of the New York legislature. But new troubles were brewing for him.

19

*By the time this 1857 issue of the* North Star *appeared, the newspaper was called simply* Frederick Douglass' Paper. *Too many other papers had the word "star" in their title.*

Anna Douglass had never taken part in her husband's work. In that way, she was very different from Douglass's business and office manager, a white woman named Julia Griffiths. Julia was involved in everything he did. The two were together so much that people began to whisper about a romance between them. William Lloyd Garrison became angry at Douglass for dragging the abolitionist movement into a scandal.

An even bigger disagreement between Douglass and Garrison concerned their views on how to end slavery. Garrison was against using force, but Douglass no longer believed Southern slave owners would ever give up their "property" on their own. Although the abolitionist movement was stronger than ever, and many abolitionists were in Congress, the slave owners showed no signs of giving in. Douglass had become a conductor on the Underground Railroad and heard many terrible stories from runaway slaves. He started to question Garrison's position against violence.

Also, he could no longer accept Garrison's political ideas. Garrison and his followers believed the North and South should split into two countries, so the slave states would have to fend for themselves. Douglass was convinced that this would leave slaves at the mercy of their owners. In May 1851, he made a speech at the annual meeting of the American Anti-Slavery Society and told of his change of feeling. That speech ended the friendship between him and Garrison.

All over the country, arguments raged about how to fight slavery. Fights broke out in states such as Kansas, which remained "undecided" about whether or not to allow slavery. It was becoming clear that there would be no peaceful solution.

## War!

In the 1850s, Douglass became friends with John Brown, a white man who had fought against slavery in Kansas. Brown believed God had sent him to free the slaves. In 1859 he told Douglass he planned to capture the federal arsenal in Harpers

Ferry, Virginia, and give the guns to slaves to fight for their freedom. Douglass tried to talk Brown out of this idea, but Brown would not change his mind.

When Brown and his followers attacked the arsenal, U.S. Marines were called in under Robert E. Lee. Many of Brown's men were killed, and he was taken prisoner. After being tried for treason, Brown was hanged.

*A year after the hanging of John Brown, Douglass was speaking at an abolitionist meeting in Boston, when an angry mob attacked. The Civil War was only one year off.*

Because Douglass had known of Brown's plan, the state of Virginia issued a warrant for his arrest. Once again, Douglass had to flee to England. But a few months later, in May 1860, news came that his youngest daughter, Annie, had died. Heartbroken, Douglass decided to return home.

When he arrived, the country was in the middle of a fierce presidential election battle. There were so many candidates that no one got a majority of the votes. The man with the most votes was Abraham Lincoln, who was against allowing slavery in new territories but had no plan to free Southern slaves.

When Lincoln was elected, the Southern states seceded, or broke off, and formed the Confederate States of America. Lincoln promised to allow slavery in the South, but when the Confederates bombed federal troops at Fort Sumter on April 12, 1861, the Civil War began.

Douglass gave many speeches calling for the president to grant all slaves their freedom. Slowly, Lincoln began to be persuaded. On New Year's Day, 1863, he issued the Emancipation Proclamation, freeing all slaves in areas not held by Union troops. Although Lincoln had not ended slavery completely, Douglass was overjoyed at this step forward.

Douglass's next battle was to get blacks accepted into the army. In 1863, Massachusetts finally allowed blacks into some regiments. Douglass urged blacks to fight. His sons Lewis and Charles were among the first to join up.

*The 55th Massachusetts Regiment was given a big hurrah when it entered Charleston, South Carolina, at the end of the Civil War.*

But the army was not fair to black soldiers. They were given less pay and worse weapons than whites, and if they were captured by Confederate troops they were often shot. Douglass stopped telling blacks to enlist. He met with President Lincoln, who promised to help. Although Lincoln did not always do as Douglass wanted, he did enough to make Douglass believe in him. The two men became warm friends, and Lincoln often asked Douglass's advice.

At last, in 1865, the South surrendered. But then Lincoln was shot and killed. Mrs. Lincoln sent Douglass one of her husband's walking sticks, a present he treasured all his life.

Some people thought that once the war to end slavery was won, Douglass's own battles were over. But he knew they were just beginning. Blacks had not yet been given citizenship or the right to vote. He would fight for their civil rights.

## A Life of Service

Douglass once again traveled around the country, speaking out for two bills that were before Congress. One would set up a Freedmen's Bureau to give poor blacks medical, educational, and financial help. The other would give blacks all the rights of citizens, including the right to vote.

The new president, Andrew Johnson, was against both these bills, but Congress passed them into law. When some Republicans tried to keep blacks from getting more rights, Douglass spoke to them. His powerful speech turned the tide.

Finally, Congress passed the Fourteenth Amendment, which protected blacks' civil rights by making them part of the U.S. Constitution.

President Johnson then asked Douglass to head the Freedmen's Bureau. But Douglass could not bring himself to serve

*This print celebrates the passage of the Fifteenth Amendment, which enforced blacks' right to vote. Anti-slavery hero Frederick Douglass is shown (top, center).*

under a president he did not trust. Instead, he went on giving speeches about the rights of blacks and women, and he became editor of another newspaper for blacks, the *New National Era*. After his house in Rochester burned down in 1872, he moved to Washington, D.C., and worked harder than ever for the cause of freedom. He wanted to make sure that the country elected presidents who cared about blacks' rights.

Then Douglass became head of the Freedmen's Savings and Trust Company, a bank that tried to help blacks. But the bank was in bad shape. Although Douglass lent the bank his own money, it had to shut down.

Finally, in 1877, President Rutherford B. Hayes made Douglass the marshal of Washington, D.C. It was the highest job a black had ever held in the U.S. government.

## The Final Years

In 1882, Anna Douglass died after a long illness. Douglass was very sad, but he went on working and writing in the beautiful twenty-room house he had bought near Washington. Then, in early 1884, he married a white woman named Helen Pitts. This upset some of his admirers among both blacks and whites. But he and his new wife were very happy together.

In 1889, President Benjamin Harrison offered Douglass the

job of minister to Haiti. The Haitians were honored to have such a great man among them, and Douglass tried to help them free themselves from poverty. But when the United States wanted to put a naval base in Haiti, and the Haitians refused, Douglass would not put pressure on them. That made some Americans angry.

By 1891 the heat and humidity in Haiti were making Douglass ill, so he returned to the United States. There he spoke out about the lynching of blacks in the South.

On February 20, 1895, Douglass went to a women's rights meeting. As the white-haired, still handsome man walked to the platform, the whole crowd cheered him, calling out his name. That night, while he was proudly telling Helen what had happened, he had a heart attack and died. He was seventy-seven years old.

All over America, people mourned him. Hundreds went to the church in Washington, D.C., where he lay in state, to pay their last respects. Afterward, his wife and children took his body to Rochester to be buried. To many people, black and white, he himself had been the North Star, showing them the way to freedom.

## IMPORTANT EVENTS IN THE LIFE OF FREDERICK DOUGLASS

1817   Frederick Augustus Washington Bailey is born in February on a plantation in Tuckahoe, Maryland.

1838   Frederick escapes to the North. He changes his name to Frederick Douglass and marries Anna Murray.

1841   Douglass speaks before a group of abolitionists in Nantucket, Massachusetts. He sets out on a speaking tour.

1845   Douglass publishes his autobiography, *Narrative of the Life of Frederick Douglass.*

1847   Douglass founds an anti-slavery newspaper called the *North Star.*

1861–1865   Douglass helps recruit blacks for the Union Army.

1882   Anna Douglass dies. Two years later, Frederick Douglass marries Helen Pitts.

1889–1891   Douglass serves as minister to Haiti.

1895   On February 20, Frederick Douglass dies. He is buried in Rochester, New York.

# FIND OUT MORE ABOUT FREDERICK DOUGLASS

*Frederick Douglass: The Black Lion* by Patricia and Fredrick McKissack (Chicago: Childrens Press, 1987).

*Frederick Douglass Fights for Freedom* by Margaret Davidson (New York: Scholastic, 1989).

*Frederick Douglass: Leader Against Slavery* by Patricia and Fredrick McKissack (Hillside, N.J.: Enslow Publishers, 1991).

*Slave and Citizen: The Life of Frederick Douglass* by Nathan Irvin Huggins (Boston: Little, Brown, 1980).

*Young Frederick Douglass: Fight for Freedom* by Laurence Santrey (Mahwah, N.J.: Troll Associates, 1983).

*Facing page:*
*Douglass with his second wife, Helen.*
*His niece, Eva Pitts, stands behind them.*

# INDEX